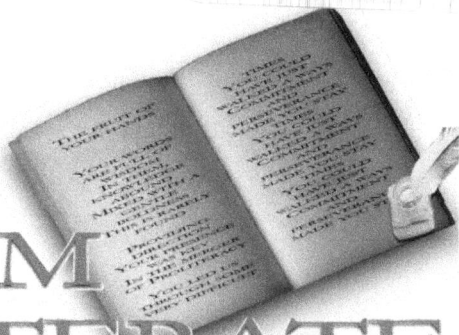

FROM
ILLITERATE
TO POET

EARL MILLS

Published By:
Jasher Press & Co.
www.jasherpress.com
P.O. Box 14520
New Bern, NC 28561

From Illiterate to Poet
Copyright© 2011 to Earl Mills
Interior Text Design by Pamela S. Almore
Cover Design by Pamela S. Almore

ISBN: 978-0615513539

First Edition
Printed and bound in the United States of America

FROM ILLITERATE TO POET

EARL MILLS

JASHER PRESS & CO.

I dedicate this book to my wife Marie.

During our thirty-nine years of marriage, you have always had my back, standing by my side with words of encouragement and never belittling me because of my inability to read.

Your constant support has made the journey from illiterate to poet

possible.

Table of Contents

Hi. My name is Edward Earl Mills.

The poem titled "Squirrels" is the first poem I remember writing. I was in the seventh grade. My teacher asked the class to write a story or poem. Being from the country, the idea of squirrels came to mind. She thought it was a good poem. It came fairly easily to me. From then till 1993, I only wrote a few rhyming lines. Later that year, I wrote "Stop the Killing, Color," which is now titled "The Color I Am, and Can I Be Your Friend." The remainder of my poems were written in the last seven years, after I learned to read.

Here are some poems-from the poet who could not read.

THE REST OF MY LIFE

What are you doing for the rest of my life-
Beautiful lady, friend, lover and wife?

Let's go dancing in God's moonlight,
Holding hands until dawn is bright.

When we kiss, it's like there's no tomorrow.
It takes away my hurt, pain, and sorrow.

Let's hold each other and cuddle tight
On a long, cold winter night.

Let's run through the meadow as we walk through life.
There's nothing we can't accomplish as husband and wife.

My life has been enriched,
My heart held at bay,
When we are together
In that special way.

From Illiterate To Poet

Help me to hear what your heart has to say.
I'm not being selfish, wanting my way.

Allowing each of us to be ourselves-
Giving to each other till there's nothing left.

Whether together or apart,
The other's well-being is always at heart.

Spending time doing nothing with you
Always makes me happy, not blue.

When I am old and you are, too,
I hope that I still stir these emotions in you.

&

AFTER ALL THESE YEARS

After all these years, my heart still flutters.
Now and again, my name you utter.

I see you in the faces of the children we've raised
Every time I take a gaze.

A wife, friend, and lover-
Why would one look for another?

On your encouragement I can depend
When I need it time and again.

In times of joy, we laugh.
When I am wrong, you tell me-
A better man you want me to be.

Smiles like sunshine,
Hugs of gold-
Thinking of you,
I'll never grow old.

From Illiterate To Poet

When nothing is on my mind,
My thoughts are of you.
Oh, what a lovely view!

I look inside myself-I see
A bit of you, a bit of me.
How can this be?

Times come and go.
People change with the wind.
On this you can depend-
Lovers until the end.

Kisses of honey with lips so divine,
Oh, what a wonder-this lady of mine.
In front of the fireplace, flickers and flames,
All along, I whisper your name.

You're wearing nothing-you wear it well.
Inside of me, my emotions swell.
Your passion is unbridled,
My heart is smitten,

For what happens next has yet to be written.

❧

DIPLOMA IN HAND

Graduated from high school, diploma in hand.
Why I received it, I don't understand.
With mixed emotions, I held it high,
Knowing within that it was a lie.

The words that were written, to me, were Greek.
Nevertheless, a job I must seek.
Busy with life as years go by.
Tears in my heart I wanted to cry.
Now married, the children came.
Having to raise them-who's to blame?

Reached out for help-at first I failed.
Disheartened inside-who can I tell?
Somehow within, a planted seed,
A call for help-I've learned to read!
Diploma in hand, I lift it high.
No tears in my heart, no longer do I cry.

∞

From Illiterate To Poet

From Illiterate To Poet

TWENTY-SIX LETTERS

Befuddled by the alphabet-
Fifty years old and can't read yet.
Twenty-six letters have brought me shame.
Someone asked me to spell my name.
Another bulletin at work today-
Who can I ask, "What does it say?"
"Grandpa, will you read this book to me?"
I tell her the letters are too small to see.

I don't have my glasses, I'm running late-
I am a victim to this lie I hate.
Cannot read-won't tell a soul.
Secrets of my youth-now I am old.
Letter after letter I can't figure out.
Frustration inside-a silent shout.
Twenty-six letters can raise so much hell.
They have secrets to me they will not tell.

This secret locked within-
I will not let these letters win.

ℬↄ

From Illiterate To Poet

A CHILD LEFT BEHIND

I take a seat in the back of the class.
If I'm called on, I hope that it's last.
A grade behind, my friends are gone-
Another reason to feel alone.

I think I'm dumb. How stupid I must be.
Everyone in the world can read except me!
I wonder if I should tell my closest friend.
Will they use it to do me in?

Just passed a note by a
cute girl in class-
Can't read the first word,
nor the last.
My grade indicates I'll be
left behind-
Another adult in the
welfare line.

My parents, teachers, and
school-why can't they see?

From Illiterate To Poet

Why is this problem left to a child like me?
The bell rings. I sigh, thanking GOD for day's end.
Tomorrow, hours of anguish until this time again.
I cry aloud in silence this day
In hope that help will come my way.

&

LORD, I NOW CONFESS

I have tried. I've made a mess.
To you, oh Lord, I now confess.

I listened and heard the Word each day.
Now and then, I'd even pray.

As night gives way to dawn's first light,
Lord, fill my soul. I will not fight.

Step by step, I need your grace.
Come now, Lord, and fill this space.

❧

From Illiterate To Poet

MY ALMOST-NEW CHRISTMAS BIKE

He found a chain,
Sand and oiled it a bit.
With tender loving care,
He made it fit.

After a hard day's work,
On it he'd work awhile,
In anticipation
Of my Christmas Day smile.

I can't remember what my seven
Other siblings got for Christmas that year.
But when I think about that bike,
To my eyes it brings a tear.

For a man that worked too hard,
For the few dollars that he received,
Could not have known the impression
An almost-new bike would leave.

From Illiterate To Poet

He straightened the rim,
A tube he'd have to patch.
A fender here and there
He would try to match.

Chrome and spray-painted parts
Sparkle and shine.
It wasn't new,
But I didn't mind.

Christmas is about love,
Not things.
It's the joy
That an almost new bike can bring.

&

THE DOG HOUSE

I go there more than I like.
The walls I am familiar with-
Every cranny and crack.
When I leave, there is no need to worry, for I will be back.

Every time I go there, I say it's my last-
Got to make this doghouse a thing of the past.

How I get there, I don't understand.
Why am I here? I am the man.

I've got a good mind to go and get her straight.
But this might mean more time in the place that I hate.

Not built with wood, brick, or hand-

Year after year, it still stands.

From Illiterate To Poet

This is one house that should be condemned.
We'd build it back, for hindsight is dim.

It has no boundaries, generational nor race.
My father spoke of it. My son has filled its space.

Stubbornness, no forgiveness, and selfishness
Have made its foundation strong.
Neither one of us will admit that we're wrong.

This last verse is written from the house,
Trying to figure out how to get back with my
spouse.

ॐ

MOTHER'S CARE

Words seem inadequate as I try to express
A mother's love and tenderness.

The extra mile when walked in
love is but a step away-
The steps you have taken each
and every day.

Mothers do what they have to do
When they are doing it for you.

Through good times and bad,
Happy and sad,
Laughs and frowns,
Ups and downs,
You are always there.
I know you care.

From Illiterate To Poet

The ways of the Lord were instilled in me
By the way you live your life-
Those things a wise man looks for when they take a
wife.

The extra mile isn't that far
When the love of a child is what she's going for.

A comforting voice, a listening ear,
A shoulder to cry on is always near.

She tells me I'm wrong when others lie.
My heart is broken when I make her cry.

A mother's love for her child
Will always go the extra mile.

ଚ

ALONE WITH MYSELF

With guard down, I sigh-
Alone with myself, no need to lie.

All hypocritical thoughts now rest-
No one to impress.

Sunday's face put aside-
I do not run, I cannot hide.

Society dictates how I should act.
Only God knows what I am like.

All alone with myself,
The one I know best-
Naked before God, I now rest.

❧

From Illiterate To Poet

HAND IN HAND

Today is the day for lovers all over the world.
I stand in awe that you are my girl.

Today I pledge my love so true.
My life I will to spend with you.

Hand in hand, we walk this life.
Oh, the joy-with you as my wife.

Life's many tomorrows, no matter the task-
Hand in hand, it shall pass.

BE MY VALENTINE

ଓ

From Illiterate To Poet

LIKE UNTO A FATHER

Without a word, your life has spoken,
Ringing loudly in my soul.

Things I thought would never be
In my life now unfold.

From Illiterate To Poet

MOTHER

When the sound of nothing echoes loud,
I see her face in every cloud.

Soon to pass away-
Still, memories seem to stay.

In every whistling wind,
Every now and then, I hear her.

Rustling leaves and cracking thunder-
A quiet still voice makes me wonder.

As trees bring forth their fruit in season,
In that, I see a mother's reason.

From Illiterate To Poet

Here today, gone tomorrow-
I miss you so. Can't you feel my sorrow?

In her words, I hear the wisdom of generations gone by.
Mothers teaching children-no longer will they cry.

With loving care, her arms stretch forth
Like branches of a tree.
For in them, there is a peace-
A place you'd like to be.

A broken heart her words will heal,
For in her soul that will she feel.

In wakened hours and un-thought thoughts,
You're on my mind today.
Going out and coming in my mind
Is never far away.

Listen-can you hear the sound? It is in the air.
It is love and understanding. She will always care.

છ

STOP THE KILLING

Brothers, let's stop the killing.
For to us, the short straw we are dealing.
Killing one another has never been right.
Let's join together, and this we can fight.

Open your ears and hear the cry
Before another brother has to die.
What happened to peace,
Love, and brotherhood-
Helping one another
For the world's common good?

Why do we have to destroy ourselves-
Killing one another,
Until there's no one left?
The black man-his oppressions are deep.
Don't let the anger of our oppressions
Make another mother weep.
The only one that can stop us is us.
Let's get together, and this we can discuss.

જી

From Illiterate To Poet

LEAVES

Today, just a bud–
Until autumn colors it,
Then falls where it may.

From Illiterate To Poet

CONFORMING TO HIS LIKENESS

If you want to conform to the likeness of Christ,
You must be obedient throughout your life.

Don't take your compassion and put it on a shelf.
Show love to your brother, and not just yourself.

If you want to be faithful in the face of temptation,
Apply the Word of God in every situation.

Humility is essential in your life.
It changes your character to the likeness of Christ.

Build your obedience.
Build up your faith.
Build your compassion.
Keep the devil in his place.

ॐ

From Illiterate To Poet

THE FRUIT OF YOUR HANDS

Your words are full of wisdom
In them, knowledge abound
Mixed with a gentle boldness
This is rarely found

Providing direction
Your presence was key
In the merger of Proliteracy

You led us through some very difficult times
You could have just walked a ways
Commitment and perseverance made you stay

Rises while it is yet night
Not eating the bread of idleness
Seeking and willingly working hard.
Has brought you great success

From Illiterate To Poet

An alumna of Harvard
Graduate of Queen's
But the love for your husband and sons
Is what fulfills your dreams

You have helped plow new ground
Planting seeds in the hearts of adult learners
In every nation and tongue
Giving us a voice
With that voice
We will declare
"THAT WE ARE"

You have a different way of phrasing thing
With a Canadian twist
People love these Shanisms
Can you imagine this

We have been the recipients
Of what determination can do
We will forever
Be indebted to you

&

SHE TOILS FOR OTHERS

Dawn, not yet! The un-oiled hinge squeaks,
Echoing through a silhouette of light of Mother's shadow
Cast upon her children's faces.
Just another day like all the rest. She leaves to toil for others,
Leaving her own to subsist for themselves.

As her hand turns the knob of the back door,
Her only bestowed entrance,
The cascade of light scintillating through windows not yet cleaned
Shows the pain in the hands
That changes the diapers of children not of her loins.

On tender knees from midnight prayer,
She cleans scuff marks of shoes that care not.
As the sun touches the tree tops,
Tender hands turn the knob of the front door.
The not-yet-oiled hinge squeaks.

A smile replaces the painted-on one worn all day.
Now, another day's work ahead-
Not of toil, for it is her own.

ॐ

From Illiterate To Poet

I STAND IN AWE

With every heartbeat and breath I take,

I stand in awe when I awake.

&

From Illiterate To Poet

DEVIL KEEP ON BOTHER'N ME

Dat dare devil keep on bother'n me.
Done told 'em ta gwone.

Don't do dem thangs no mo.
Done went and got myself rebone.

Gwanna go to chuch dis here sundee.
Gwanna praze 'Em all day long.

Devil ain't my massa no mo.
Done told 'em ta gwone.

$\wp$

From Illiterate To Poet

THE COLOR I AM

A man is a man-nothing more, nothing less.
Let's give the color thing a much-needed rest.
I pray for the day that color we can no longer see,
And a man's race will no longer matter to me.

From the young to the old,
Ending racism should be everyone's goal.
The color that you are was not your choice.
It was chosen by God's Heavenly voice.

Red, yellow, black, white-
What is it about me that you don't like?

We've got to look deep within,
Past the color of one's skin.
Why does a man's pigmentation
Control the outcome of his situation?

From Illiterate To Poet

All mankind-some good, some bad.
We're in this thing together. Isn't racism sad?
They call it racism for lack of a better word.
I think that it is a sickness, from what I have heard.

I'm black, you're white-
Who's wrong, who's right?
Men are many colors on this planet Earth.
But should it really matter? The inside carries his
worth.

Red, yellow, black, white-
Why can't we try to treat everyone alike?
It's not just black or white,
It's a fight for what's right.

ဆ

LUKEWARM

Here I am again, Lord,
Hands lifted high.
In your sanctuary,
My heart tells the lie.

Another week
I've robbed you, God.
A bill fell due.
Now, with hands lifted high,
Thoughts are of You.

Bible untouched
For yet another day-
Until Sunday,
It shall stay.

From Illiterate To Poet

Start to pray,
Mind drifts away,
Filled with toils
Of the day.

Things I do
Dishonor You-
Unclean thoughts
Through and through.

My vows I renew.
Lord, cleanse me
That I may worship
Only You.

&

SQUIRRELS

Squirrels make their nests in the hallows of trees
Out of different kinds of leaves.

In the fall, they gather nuts while they're brown.
In the fall, they laugh and frown.

The squirrels that live in town
Are protected all around.

They can hop from limb to limb
With no one shouting after them.

∞

From Illiterate To Poet

GOD SENT

God looked down through eternity to this place and time,
For He knew that in you, the jewels He would find.

Setting events into motion that would shape your lives
Long before you were husband and wife.

You were placed in eternity for a time that was right,
Here at Dayspring to show forth His light.

Dayspring's vision in your hearts is clear.
Getting us to see has brought forth a tear.

In the midst of adversity, you're anchored in His love,
Knowing that your strength comes from above.

Your lives have spoken, ringing loudly in our souls,
Planting seeds that forever will unfold.

God's wisdom abides in your daily conversations,
And it is applied in every situation.

In you we see yielded vessels, conduits of His Word,
For His still quiet voice you have surely heard.

God blesses us when He blesses you,
Because giving of yourselves is what you do.

❧

From Illiterate To Poet

AS I TELL YOU THAT I LOVE YOU ONCE AGAIN

As I look upon the Heavens,
And I tell you that I love you once again,

Everything within me now joins my heart in praise,
As I tell you that I love you once again.

With my hands lifted high, I cannot deny,
As I tell you that I love you once again.

All things around me become shadows in your light,
And your spirit within me rejoices in your might,
As I tell you that I love you once again.

&

MARIE, WHEN I LOOK AT YOU!

In our journey of thirty-eight years,
The good and bad we have faced.
Together, walking hand-in-hand
Has brought us to this place.

When I look at you,
It still happens.
I get all bubbly inside,
Like the day you became my
bride.

You are my encourager.
You always had my back,
Even when I've done things
That you didn't like.

I am captivated by your beauty.

To you, the years have been kind.
From the gentleness of your lips,
To that subtle sway of your hips,
To the brilliance of your mind,
To my delight, this thing I find.

From Illiterate To Poet

Your eyes carry warmness
That melts my sometimes selfish heart.
So I give myself to you,
Each and every part!

Your integrity guides your steps.
Nonsense you will not accept.
Your inner strength comes from above,
Which gives you your endless love.

Lisa, Donavon, Rhonda, Netasha, and Bradley,
These, our children, you do for gladly.

Your beauty takes my breath away.
In your embrace is where I long to stay.

છ

A DREAM

A dream is an uncultivated possibility.
When left alone,
This dream will fill
The cemetery of our lands.

If nurtured,
It will surpass the limitations
Of our imaginations.

෩

From Illiterate To Poet

MOVE A GRAIN OF SAND

A steady drip will fill a bucket.
If you feel like you can't move a mountain,
Move a grain of sand.

❧

From Illiterate To Poet

THE BACK DOOR

No word had to be spoken.
Its message was crystal clear.
Generation after generation
Would have to enter here.

The back door was so hard to open,
For it held the belittlement of my kind.
It shackled our will, our souls and our minds.

The back door was designed,
Engineered, and put in place.
Its purpose was to dishonor,
Belittle and disgrace,
So that we would never
Forget our place. In silence, it spoke loudly.
Its message still rings today.
Although the front door is available,
Lingering memories seem to stay.

From Illiterate To Poet

My father entered that door in shame,
Holding my hand.
I searched my heart, mind, and soul.
I did not understand.

The hurt painted a picture
On my father's face.
Will it ever be erased?

As we stand here now,
With faded memories,
Will we ever forget?
Have the seeds that they planted
Fully matured yet?

છ૦

THIS PRAISE

From the top of my voice, I will praise you.
You're the one that saved me.
You're the one that gave me "this praise."

You lifted me from my sin.
Now "this praise" comes from within.
To you alone, I give "this praise."

From Illiterate To Poet

IF YOU CONFESS

No matter what in life you've done,
It's covered by the blood of God's only Son.

If you believe this in your heart,
And with your mouth you confess,

In His love,
You'll find rest.

From Illiterate To Poet

MY NAME IS ILLITERATE

I'm red, yellow, black and white.
From every nation and tongue,
Old, middle-aged, and young.
I have no boundaries, generational nor race.
My father couldn't read. Now I take his place.
You look for me in all the wrong places.
For I'm closer than you think.
Sitting in the church pew,
Pretending to read just like you.
Hidden in plain sight,
Woven into the fabric of society,
Because of my one ignorance.
Masquerading as literate
Has become my game,
Because of the shame
Of my real name.

From Illiterate To Poet

Avoiding situations
In fear of hearing this word.
READ-that which I cannot do.
Many try to give me a face
With social status or race.
I'm just ordinary people
That cannot read.
Embarrassment keeps me from coming to you.
Normally, it takes a tragedy
For me to break through.
I've tried to paint a picture

On the canvas of your mind,

To help you understand

This illiterate life of mine.

૪૭

YOU HUNGER AND THIRST

Dawn is now.

His gentle voice awakens the praise that's due.

A hunger that burns within to praise Him more each

day,

Longing for His presence.

His Word is birthed in you.

∽

From Illiterate To Poet

ONLY GOD CAN COUNT THE APPLES IN A SEED

Anyone can count the seeds in an apple.

Only God can count the apples in a seed.

When you teach someone to read,

You plant a seed.

&

From Illiterate To Poet

TRUE TO MYSELF

To others I may lie.

To myself I know why.

Hidden secrets never told.

Taken to my grave.

Truth locked within.

One knows, not a friend.

This thing I must let go.

It carries my woe.

I tell myself I know.

Secrets are now gone.

No longer do I groan.

To myself I do not lie.

൙

From Illiterate To Poet

EVERY NOW AND THEN

Every now and then,
A person comes along
That will give themselves
To God, and God alone.

We have been recipients
Of what happens when we do.
For God's blessings surely flow through you.

Hours spent in reverence
Have brought you to this place.
More and more,
You long to seek His face.

From Illiterate To Poet

His wisdom abides
In your conversation.
It is applied
In every situation.

It has enriched our lives,
Strengthening us to stand.
You're a yielded vessel
In the Master's hands.

A SHEPHERD'S LOVE

The Word of God is your foundation.
On it, you firmly stand.
Not by power, nor by might,
But by God's spirit you can.

With a firm but gentle voice,
And wisdom beyond your years,
You lead, you guide, you care,
And you put asunder all fear.

You lead by example.
Your words bring life.
It's seen day after day
In the people, your son, and your wife.

She stands beside you, strong but gentle.
The purpose is the same.
To lift up His name,
No glory, no fame.

From Illiterate To Poet

Many hats you wear today
Until we take our place.
Soon, the vision given
Will stare us in the face.

I take a glimpse ahead.
I see the people instead.
A people who love, a people of joy,
A people who worship only the Lord.

ა

HE'S TEACHING ME TO BE A MAN

At dawn's first peak, familiar sounds and faint whispers fill the air.
He teaching me to be a man. It is in His prayer.

His walk is tall, shoulders back.
Not in pride. Confidence-there is no lack.

I watched Him hold my mother's hand.
He's teaching me to be a Man.

Not so much by spoken Word, but how He walks each day.
I wonder if He knew He was teaching the way.

He very seldom raised a voice against another soul.
Not because of weakness, but meekness under control.

Not wavering-steadfast and decisive was this man.
In my youth, I could not see. Now, I understand.

He passes the torch. I've tried it on for size.
My son is watching. I can see it in His eyes.

With hope and wisdom, this path I walk each day.
I do it with prayer, for my son cometh this way.

ॐ

From Illiterate To Poet

WHEN CALLED OF GOD

When called of God, others are first.
For more of God you thirst.
Yourselves are dying to others' needs,
Continually planting seeds.

Not seeking money, glory or fame.
Only Jesus do you proclaim.
You plant, water, and watch us grow.
In our future, your labor shows.

For in our hearts are planted seeds,
Because God's vision you have received.
Though the vision to you is clear,
Bringing it to pass may require a tear.

Not seeking money, glory or fame.
Only Jesus do you proclaim.
Living by principles, you teach us well.
Through eyes of others, they can tell.

Me and I, you've tried to erase.
God in us is taking its place.

From Illiterate To Poet

Not seeking money, glory or fame.
Only Jesus do you proclaim.
Leading examples, we see that you pray,
For the knowledge of God has come your way.

With wisdom and knowledge, you teach His word.
Not from yourselves-His voice you have heard.
Hearing from God is first in your lives,
Standing together as husband and wife.

Not seeking money, glory or fame.
Only Jesus do you proclaim.
With prayer in heart, you press on each day.
The Word of God leads the way.

You've humbled yourselves time and again.
If you hadn't, where would we have been?

❧

MOTHER'S DAY

Today, the world says "Thanks" to you
For all the countless things you do.
For the blood, sweat and many tears,
For hours spent praying through the years,
For always being proud of me.
You saw what others could not see.
You changed my diapers and wiped my tears.
I watched your life. It calmed my fears.

The love that's in your voice of correction
Keeps me going in the right direction.
A voice of comfort and a firm, gentle hand,
Every situation, you understand.
You saw the gifts God placed in my soul
And nurtured them so they could unfold.
Our praises are too few and far apart
To someone who gives us their very heart.

"Thanks" seems inadequate on this special day.
To cover this debt, only love I can pay.

ॐ

From Illiterate To Poet

WHEN JESUS IS LORD

When life has tossed you to and fro,
Others would be down.
Within, there is a glow.
That is when you know.
Down to one last dime,
One cent belongs to him.
Others wouldn't do.
God's spirit leads you.

Friends-not many,
Path that leads this way,
Hours spent alone,
In His presence, will you stay?
Rising of the sun,
Bring on His praise
That guides you through the day-
Not life's toils.
God's Word lights your way.

❧

From Illiterate To Poet

THANKS FROM A STUDENT

If you think your work's in vain,
Ask me-I will proclaim.
You give and give so much each day
To help your student find his way.
Actions speak louder than words.
Your unselfish deed has been heard.
In the voices of people like me,
Ask us, and we will decree.

Thanks for not laughing when I misspelled my name.
Embarrassed already, you spared me some shame.
You're more than a tutor. You are a friend.
You've gone the extra mile time and again.
My success makes you happy.
My joy is yours, too.
For you, it's not work.
It's what volunteers do.

From Illiterate To Poet

BLIND AS A BAT

Hey, you little cat in a hat. I'm a bat.
How do you like that?
I see you down there, eyeing that rat.

That's pretty good for someone
Who's blind as a bat.
Do you have nine lives,
Or is that just a tale?

Are your eyes that keen,
Or do you rely on your smell?
Do you hate water? Is that a lie, too?
There's a lot of things I wonder about you.

I'll see you later.
How about that?
Although they say
I'm blind as a bat.

৪৩

From Illiterate To Poet

I WALKED RIGHT BY

I walked right by my friend in an unsafe act.
I was in a hurry. I would be right back.
What could happen? Just minutes-that's all.
I turned around when I heard him fall.
I should have stopped and took the time.
I walked right by a friend of mine.
The next few days were hard, you see,
Every time his children would look at me.
I should have stopped and took the time.
I walked right by his wife and children today
At his funeral, not knowing what to say.
I should have stopped and took the time.
I walked right by a friend of mine.

80

From Illiterate To Poet

I KNOW WHY HE SENT HER

Through dim eyes, fifty-six years of sunsets, yet life was
crystal clear.
You may wonder, but I know why God sent her here.
Life was fairly simple. Possessions were few.
I know why He sent her-for us to take a view.

Complaining very seldom, her lips did it pass.
Can you say the same? A question you should ask.
Taking care of her grandkids, her last dime is gone again.
You would not know it. Complaining was not her twin.

I know why He sent her to me. It's crystal clear.
Even through dim eyes, the cross is always near.
Through dim eyes, she saw life as pretty good.
They were on her Savior-that is why she could.

ॐ

From Illiterate To Poet

WITH DAZED EYES

I look with dazed eyes.
Day and night pass me by.
Mind here nor there,
God's wonder did I miss.
It will be my demise.

I would listen, but not hear.
Through dazed eyes do I peer.

Days are now many.
Look on, see what I missed.
Advice given, not received.
To myself do I cleave.

Through dazed eyes,
Right comes wrong.
Blues is my song.
My dazed eyes
Will be my demise.

ℰℭ

From Illiterate To Poet

YOU'RE LORD OF ALL

The twinkling of the stars,
The moon You hung in place,
All of the universe
Displays Your mighty grace.
From the rising of the sun
To the going down of the same,
Will my soul
Magnify Your name.

From Heaven to earth
And all it's worth,
You're Lord of all-
Lion of Judah,
Prince of Peace,
Almighty God,
Whose mercies never cease.
We lift up holy hands
Without wrath or doubt,
It is You, Lord of all,
We cannot do without.
Kingdoms rise,
Kingdoms fall,
Throughout eternity,
You're Lord of all.

From Illiterate To Poet

UNITED WE STAND

United we stand-divided we fall.
We can make a change, but it's going to take us all.
Let this be the generation that changes mankind's situation.
In a nation so great that we live, why is a helping hand so
hard to give?
Society-we cannot let it be.
The future of our society depends on you and me.
We have fought one another-now let's fight together.
This storm of indifference we can weather.
This nation can be greater.
It can happen now, and not later.
Let each man find deep down within
That everyone is his brother, no matter the color of his skin.
Why can't we all become color-blind,
Looking at one's heart, soul, and mind?
With our hands joined together, and our minds in one
accord,
We can make this a greater nation with the help of the Lord.

&

From Illiterate To Poet

HE DANCED BEFORE THE LORD

Every movement showed the pain-
The past that brought him here.
His face claimed the victory,
His eyes shed a tear.
As he danced before the Lord,
A transformation was taking place.
Every step brought him closer.
Now, face-to-face,
Dancing to the rhythm of God's heartbeat.
Shackles of the past fell to his feet.
This dance was placed in eternity
For a time that was right,
Long before we beheld
Its manifestation that night.
As all things around him
Became shadows in God's light,
He danced before the Lord.
He danced with all of his might.
As he rhythmically moved,
It captivated our souls.
Before our very eyes,
God's calling did unfold.
Each rhythm-driven movement
Our heart did understand.
We saw a yielded vessel
In the Master's hand.

Ꮽ

From Illiterate To Poet

THE POET THAT COULDN'T READ

He wrote a line
That only he could understand,
Like words from a five-year-old-
Not from a man.
The thoughts and ideas
That filled his mind
Became broken English
As he scribbled line upon line.
How can someone
Who can't read or write
Be given the gift
To put the English language to flight?
He captured the beauty
Of the heart, life, and soul.
His illiterate pen
Made them unfold.
His befuddled words
Would soon find rest,
Like the journey
To the top of a mountain crest.

FROM ILLITERATE TO POET

About the Author

Imagine marrying the love of your life, raising five children together, working for the same company for over twenty-five years, and successfully hiding the fact that you cannot read.

I graduated high school in 1971 and could not read beyond a second-grade level. My wife knew, but she was the only one who knew. I hid it from my children and my grandchildren. Then, one night, I was called on to read. My forty-four-year-old secret was about to be exposed. My wife and I had joined a local church and were now in a new member's class along with eight other people. The pastor went around the table and asked everyone to read a Scripture. My heart sank as I tried to think of some excuse I could give for not reading – I couldn't find my glasses, or I had the wrong pair of glasses, but I knew nothing would work. I stumbled through every word. My wife tried to help without looking too obvious, but it was no use. I was so embarrassed I wanted to just disappear. Right then, I knew I had to get some help.

A good friend told me about the Craven Literacy Council, so I called them immediately. They assigned me a trained tutor who patiently worked with me one-on- one and step-by-step. Four years later, at the age of forty-eight, I read my first book, "Along the Gold Rush Trail." The weight I

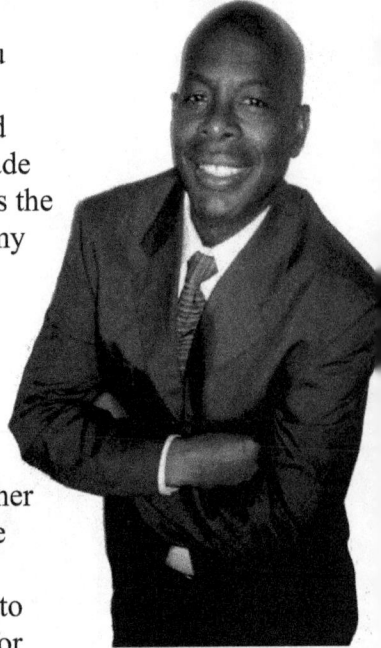

carried for over forty years had finally been lifted. It felt like someone had given me a million dollars.

Since learning to read, I have read over seventy books and novels, written over forty poems, and have been selected as a North Carolina Ambassador for Literacy. I also serve as a board member for the North Carolina Literacy Council, helping them reach out to others living under the weight of illiteracy.

I am thankful my secret was exposed, because being able to read has changed my life. It has opened a whole new world to me. I can meet new people and travel to places I have never been without leaving my home. I can read to my grandchildren and write a love poem to my wife. Most importantly, my story can inspire someone else.

FOR MORE INFORMATION ABOUT
THE AUTHOR & BOOK PURCHASES
EMILLSPOET@HOTMAIL.COM
PHONE:252.636.0778

PROLITERACY WORLDWIDE
1320 JAMESVILLE AVENUE, SYRACUSE, NY 13210
TELEPHONE: (315) 422-9121 FAX: (315) 422-6369
WWW.PROLITERACY.ORG

CRAVEN LITERACY COUNCIL
2800 NEUSE BLVD.
NEW BERN, NC 28562
TELEPHONE: (252) 637-8079
CRAVENLC@EARTHINK.NET
HTTP:/HOME.EARTHINK.NET~CRAVENLCWEB/